Christmas Cracker Jokes

Amanda Li is a writer and editor who has worked in children's publishing for many years. She lives in London with her family.

Q: What sits at her desk, arranges her pens and pencils, gets up to make coffee and eat a banana, returns to her desk, listens to *Woman's Hour* and illustrates joke books?

A: Jane Eccles!

*Also available from
Macmillan Children's Books*

The Bumper Book of Very Silly Jokes

Christmas Jokes

Football Jokes

Hot Dogs and Dinosnores:
A First Animal Joke Book

Amanda Li

Illustrated by Jane Eccles

Christmas Cracker Jokes

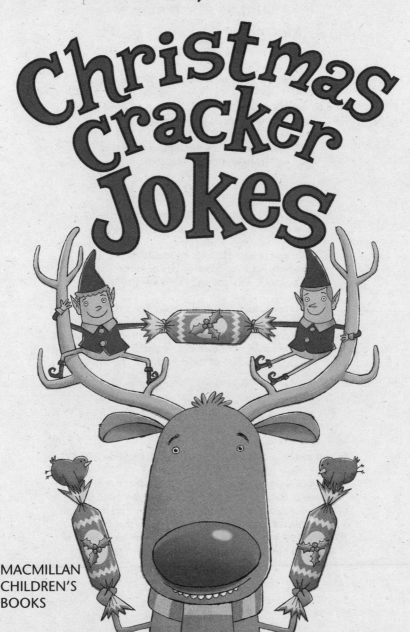

MACMILLAN
CHILDREN'S
BOOKS

Especially for my beloved Beak – J.E.

First published 2009 by Macmillan Children's Books

This edition published 2014 by Macmillan Children's Books
an imprint of Pan Macmillan
20 New Wharf Road, London N1 9RR
Associated companies throughout the world
www.panmacmillan.com

ISBN 978-1-4472-7800-9

5 7 9 8 6

A CIP catalogue record for this book is available from
the British Library.

Printed and bound by CPI Group (UK) Ltd, Croydon CR0 4YY

What's red and white and goes up and down and up and down?

Santa Claus stuck in a lift.

What's red and white, bounces and goes, 'Ho ho ho'?

Santa on a pogo stick.

What jumps from cake to cake and tastes of almonds?

Tarzipan.

What's green and white and bounces?

A spring onion.

What do vampires sing on New Year's Eve?

Auld fang syne.

What two things should you never eat before breakfast on Christmas Day?

Lunch and dinner.

Where do ghosts go for a Christmas treat?

The phantomime.

What sort of vegetables do plumbers fix?

Leeks.

**What kind of jokes does
a chiropodist like?**

Corny jokes.

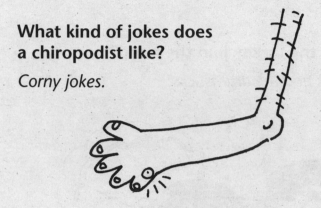

Why do bakers work so hard?

Because they need the dough.

Why did the turkey join the band?

Because it had the drumsticks.

Bryn: Did you hear the story of the three reindeer?
Gwyn: No.
Bryn: Oh dear, dear, dear.

First boy: Where does your mum come from?
Second boy: Alaska.
First boy: Don't worry, I'll ask her myself.

What's the most popular gardening magazine in the world?

Weeder's Digest.

What do you get if you cross a skeleton with a famous detective?

Sherlock Bones.

What did they call the crazy golfer?

A crack putt.

If you have a referee in football, a referee in rugby and a referee in boxing, what do you have in bowls?

Pudding.

Why did the boy throw his toast out of the window?

He wanted to see the butterfly.

What did the beaver say to the tree?

'Nice gnawing you.'

What do you call a man who's down in the mouth?

A dentist.

What does the word 'minimum' mean?

A very small mother.

**Who is the wettest married
woman in America?**

Mrs Sippi.

**Why did the chicken run on
to the football pitch?**

*Because the referee
called a foul.*

**Why didn't the skeleton go to the
New Year's Eve party?**

He had no body to go with.

What did the Christmas stocking say when it had a hole in it?

'Well, I'll be darned!'

How did the human cannonball lose his job?

He got fired.

Who wore the first shell suit?

Humpty Dumpty.

What can you touch, see and make, but cannot hold?

Your shadow.

What is long, green and goes, 'Hith, hith'?

A snake with a lisp.

Martin: Why did your dad get splinters from the book you gave him for Christmas?

Mervin: It was a logbook.

Patty: It's raining cats and dogs.

**Matty: I know, I just stepped
in a poodle.**

Why did Mickey Mouse travel into space?

He wanted to find Pluto.

If two's company and three's a crowd, what is four and five?

Nine.

Where do ships go when they are ill?

To the docks.

Dad: Would you like a pocket calculator for Christmas?

Dennis: No, thanks. I already know how many pockets I've got.

What has a trunk and is found at the North Pole?

A lost elephant.

Who earns a living driving customers away?

A taxi-driver.

Mrs Tubby: I want to buy a nice Christmas cake, please.

Confectioner: This is a nice one.

Mrs Tubby: It looks to me as if mice have nibbled it.

Confectioner: Oh no, that's impossible.

Mrs Tubby: How can you be so sure?

Confectioner: Because the cat's been lying on it all day.

What happens if you eat the Christmas decorations?

You get tinsellitis.

What do you get if you cross a shark with a snowman?

Frostbite.

What car is like a sausage?

An old banger.

Why is a turkey like an imp?

Because it's always a-gobblin'.

What goes, 'Now you see me, now you don't, now you see me, now you don't'?

A snowman walking over a zebra crossing.

Where do snowmen dance?

Snowballs.

What do you call a boy trying to get the creases out of his clothes at the North Pole?

Brrrr-ian.

Where do you find elves?

Depends where you left them.

What's the best key to get at Christmas?

A turkey.

What's green, covered with tinsel and says, 'Ribbet, ribbet'?

A mistle-toad.

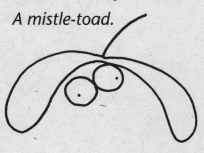

What did Mrs Claus say to Santa Claus?

'It looks like rain, dear.'

What leads you to the Christmas presents in police stations?

Santa Clues.

Who brings Christmas presents to baby sharks?

Santa Jaws.

What squeaks and is scary?

The Ghost of Christmouse Past.

What does Frosty the Snowman wear on his head?

An ice cap.

What kind of bread do elves make sandwiches with?

Shortbread.

What happens when Frosty the Snowman gets dandruff?

He gets snowflakes.

Who carries all Santa's books?

His books elf.

Who is never hungry at Christmas?

The turkey – he's always stuffed.

What do sheep say to each other at Christmas time?

'Merry Christmas to ewe.'

Why didn't Santa Claus get wet when he lost his umbrella?

It wasn't raining.

What do reindeer always say before telling you a joke?

'This one will sleigh you.'

Which of Santa's reindeer needs to mind his manners the most?

Rude-olph.

What goes, 'Ho ho ho, plop plop plop'?

Santa Claus in the toilet.

What does Frosty the Snowman eat for lunch?

Icebergers.

Why does Santa Claus go down the chimney on Christmas Eve?

Because it soots him.

What's red and white and red and white and red and white?

Santa Claus rolling down a hill.

Why did the reindeer cross the road?

Because he was tied to a chicken.

Why did the elf curl up in the fireplace?

He wanted to sleep like a log.

What nationality are Santa and Mrs Claus?

North Polish.

What can Santa give away and still keep?

A cold.

How do you tell the difference between tinned turkey and tinned custard?

Read the labels.

Elf: Santa, the reindeer swallowed my pencil. What should I do?

Santa: Use a pen.

What kind of bills do elves have to pay?

Jingle bills.

How does Frosty the Snowman get around?

On an ice-icle.

If Santa Claus and Mrs Claus had a child, what would he be called?

A subordinate clause.

How long should an elf's legs be?

Just long enough to reach the ground.

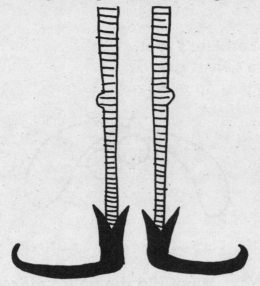

Who is Frosty the Snowman's favourite aunt?

Aunt Arctica.

A boy went to the butcher's and saw that the turkeys were ninety pence a pound. He asked the butcher, 'Do you raise them yourself?'

'Of course I do,' the butcher replied. 'They were only fifty pence a pound this morning!'

**If athletes get athlete's foot,
what do Santa's elves get?**

Mistle-toes.

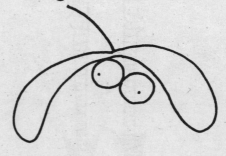

**What did the police officer
say when he saw Frosty
the Snowman stealing?**

'Freeze!'

What do they call a wild elf in Texas?

Gnome on the range.

What did the sheep say to the shepherd?

'Season's bleatings.'

What kind of pine has the sharpest needles?

A porcupine.

How do elves greet one another?

'Small world, isn't it?'

What do you get if you cross a bell with a skunk?

Jingle smells.

What does Frosty the Snowman drink?

Iced tea.

What did the elf say when he was teaching Santa Claus to use the computer?

'First, yule log in!'

What did the snowman's wife give him when she was angry with him?

The cold shoulder.

What fish only swims at night?

A starfish.

What does Santa use when he goes fishing?

His North Pole.

What do ghosts put on their turkey at Christmas?

Grave-y.

Why are fish so smart?

Because they live in schools.

What should you give a sick bird?

Tweetment.

Why can't a leopard hide?

Because he's always spotted.

What dog loves to take bubble baths?

A shampoodle.

What time does a duck wake up?

At the quack of dawn.

Where does Frosty the Snowman keep his money?

In a snow bank.

What did the dog say when he sat on sandpaper?

'Ruff.'

Why was Santa's little helper depressed?

He had low elf-esteem.

What would you do if an elephant sat in front of you in the cinema?

Miss most of the film.

Why do elves scratch themselves?

Because they're the only ones who know where they're itchy.

45

**Why does Santa Claus owe
everything to the elves?**

Because he is an elf-made man.

**What's red and white and
gives presents to gazelles?**

Santelope.

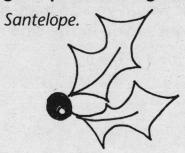

What does Frosty the Snowman take when he gets sick?

A chill pill.

What goes, 'Ho Ho Swoosh!? Ho Ho Swoosh!'?

Santa in a revolving door.

How do rabbits keep their hair in place?

With hare-spray.

**What kind of gum
do bees chew?**

Bumble-gum.

**What did Adam
tell his girlfriend
on 24 December?**

'It's Christmas, Eve.'

What does Tarzan sing at Christmas time?

Jungle Bells.

How do you make an idiot laugh on New Year's Eve?

Tell him a joke on Christmas Day.

WAITING ROOM

Why did the Christmas cake go to the doctor?

Because he was feeling crummy.

Where is the best place to put your Christmas tree?

Between your Christmas two and your Christmas four.

Knock, knock.
Who's there?
Mary.
Mary who?
Mary Christmas!

What do you get if you cross an apple with a Christmas tree?

A pineapple.

Why do people cry at Christmas time?

Because they are santa-mental.

Knock, knock.
Who's there?
Holly.
Holly who?
Holly-days are here again!

'Waiter, what's this fly doing in my soup?'
'The breaststroke, sir.'

'Waiter, there are two flies in my soup!'

'Don't worry, sir, we won't charge you for the extra one.'

'Waiter, there's a flea in my soup!'

'Shall I tell him to hop it, sir?'

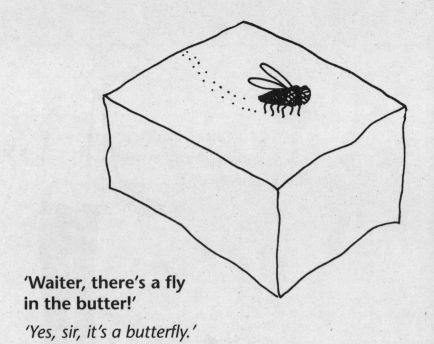

'**Waiter, there's a fly
in the butter!**'

'*Yes, sir, it's a butterfly.*'

**What falls down all the time at the
North Pole, but never hurts itself?**

Snow.

'Waiter, do you serve snails?'

'Yes, sir, we serve anyone that comes in.'

What do angry mice send each other in December?

Cross-mouse cards.

How do you get a baby astronaut to sleep?

Rocket.

'Waiter, will my pizza be long?'

'No, sir, it will be round!'

'Thanks for the electric guitar you gave me for Christmas,' Timmy said to his uncle. 'It's the best present I ever got.'

'That's great,' said his uncle. 'Do you know how to play it?'

'Oh, I don't play it. My mum gives me seven pounds a week not to play it during the day, and my dad gives me five pounds a week not to play it at night!'

What Christmas carol is popular in the desert?

O Camel Ye Faithful.

What's the best present for someone who likes to play it cool?

A combined fridge and CD player.

Gemma: First the good news – Mum gave me a goldfish for Christmas.

Emma: What's the bad news?

Gemma: I get the bowl next Christmas.

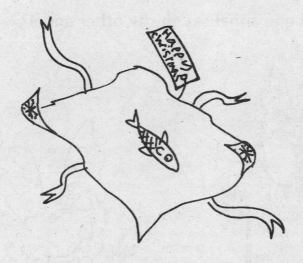

Which goalkeeper can jump higher than a crossbar?

All of them – a crossbar can't jump.

What did one angel say to the other angel?

'Halo there.'

Lizzie: Mum, do you remember that plate Granny gave you last Christmas that you were so worried we might break?

Mother: Yes.

Lizzie: Well, your worries are over.

'Why do elephants paint their toenails red?'

'So that they can hide in cherry trees.'

'Don't be silly – elephants don't hide in cherry trees!'

'Haven't you ever seen one in a cherry tree?'

'No.'

'Proves how good the disguise is then, doesn't it?'

Shane: How are you getting on with the guitar your dad gave you for Christmas?

Wayne: Oh, I threw it away.

Shane: Why did you do that?

Wayne: It had a hole in the middle.

Little Belinda was given a bottle of perfume and a recorder for Christmas. Her parents' rather pompous friends arrived for lunch on Boxing Day and, as the family sat down at the table, Belinda confided to them, 'If you smell a little smell and hear a little noise, it's me.'

Cake Chuckles

For Emily's birthday, her friends decided to get together and make her a very unusual cake. It was a savoury cake with a bread base, lots of cheese on top and bits of ham and mushroom sprinkled all over it. At her birthday party they brought it out for her as a surprise, and Emily was absolutely delighted. She was also very hungry and she scoffed the lot.

'Wow!' she said, as she finished the last piece. 'That must have been really hard to make.'

'Oh no,' said her friends. 'It was a pizza cake.'

How do we know that carrots are good for the eyes?

Have you ever seen a rabbit wearing glasses?

Ben: Did you like the dictionary I gave you for Christmas?

Len: Yes, I've been trying to find the words to thank you.

What do you call a little lobster who won't share his toys?

Shellfish.

Mrs Feather: How much are those teddy bears?

Shop assistant: Nine pounds the pair or five pounds for one.

Mrs Feather: Here's four pounds – I'll have the other one.

Dad: What have you got your eye on for Christmas?

Dennis: I've got my eye on that shiny red bike in the shop in the high street.

Dad: Well, you'd better keep your eye on it, because you'll never get your bottom on it.

Man in shop: I'm trying to buy a present for my wife. Can you help me out?

Shop assistant: Certainly, sir. Which way did you come in?

Mrs Fiver: Have you any crocodile shoes?

Shop assistant: Certainly, madam, what size feet does your crocodile have?

Annie: What does Santa do in the summer?

Danny: He's a gardener.

Annie: How do you know that?

Danny: Because he's always saying,
'Hoe hoe hoe.'

Why did Santa spring back up the chimney?

To try out his new jumpsuit.

What do Santa's elves have for tea?

Fairy cakes.

Why should you never invite a team of footballers for dinner?

Because they're always dribbling.

**What's red and white, goes,
'Ho ho ho,' and spins round and round?**

Santa in a washing machine.

Why is Santa's nose in the middle of his face?

Because it's the scenter.

Where was Santa when the lights went out?

In the dark.

What happened when Santa's dog ate garlic?

His bark was worse than his bite.

**What's the best time
to buy a budgie?**

When they're going cheap.

**What happened when Mrs Santa served soap
flakes instead of cornflakes for breakfast?**

Santa was so angry he foamed at the mouth.

**What kind of coat does Santa wear
when it's raining on Christmas Eve?**

A wet one.

What do you call a donkey with three legs?

A wonkey.

What's an ig?

An Eskimo house without a loo.

What did the north wind say to the east wind?

'Let's play draughts.'

What did the boy say to the girl when they met at the North Pole?

'What's an ice girl like you doing in a place like this?'

What's a mushroom?

A place where Eskimos keep their huskies.

How do rabbits travel?

By hare plane.

What's the difference between a fish and a piano?

You can't tuna fish.

Santa travels in a sleigh. What do elves travel in?

Minivans!

Waiter, waiter, my turkey has gone off!

Which way did it go?

Why are Christmas trees like bad knitters?

They both drop their needles!

Why do cows lie down when it's raining?

To keep each udder dry.

How deep is the water in a pond full of frogs?

Knee-deep, knee-deep, knee-deep.

What does a toad say when he sees something he likes?

'That's toad-ally awesome!'

Dumb Donald: I'd like to buy a puppy for my brother. How much are they?
Pet-shop owner: Twenty-five pounds apiece.
Dumb Donald: How much is a whole one?

Where do wasps go when they're sick?

To the waspital.

What's black and white and blue?

A freezing-cold zebra.

Jane: I wish I could afford to buy a pedigree puppy for Christmas.
Wayne: Why do you want a pedigree puppy?
Jane: Oh, I don't want one. I just wish I had enough money to buy one.

Have you heard the joke about the wall?

I'd tell you but you'd never get over it.

On which side of Santa's face is his beard?

The outside.

What happens if you kiss a clock?

Your lips tick.

What do mermaids spread on their toast?

Merma-lade.

What do you call an elf who steals gift wrap from the rich and gives it to the poor?

Ribbon Hood.

**What is twenty feet tall, has sharp
teeth and goes, 'Ho ho ho'?**

Tyranno-santa rex!

How did Rudolph learn to read?

He was elf-taught.

Why was the biscuit sad?

*Because his mother had
been a wafer so long.*

What did the dog say to the bone?

'Nice gnawing you.'

85

Who's the world's most famous water spy?

James Pond.

Why did Piglet peer into the toilet?

He was looking for Pooh.

Who flies through the air in his underwear?

Peter Pants.

Who is the smelliest fairy in the world?

Stinkerbell.

**Who is huge, green and refuses
to speak to anyone?**

The Incredible Sulk.

What's yellow and brown and hairy?

Cheese on toast on the carpet.

Knock, knock.
Who's there?
Rabbit.
Rabbit who?
Rabbit up neatly, it's a present.

Knock, knock.
Who's there?
Boo.
Boo who?
There's no need to cry.

Knock, knock.
Who's there?
Ketchup.
Ketchup who?
Ketchup with me if you can.

Knock, knock.
Who's there?
Cargo.
Cargo who?
Car go beep beep.

Batty Books

Walking in the Rain **by Miss D. Bus**

How to Get Rich **by Robin Banks**

The World's Worst Cow Jokes **by Terry Bull**

What to Do When School Is Closed **by Holly Day**

Cooking Outdoors **by Barbie Cue**

The Haunted House **by Hugo First**

Winning at Games **by Vic Tree**

How to Do Magic Tricks **by Abby Cadabra**

Cheeses of the World **by E. Dam**

Time for Lunch **by Dean R. Bell**

What did one candle say to the other?

'Are you going out tonight?'

What did one volcano say to the other volcano?

'I lava you!'

What did the pencil sharpener say to the pencil?

'Stop going in circles and get to the point.'

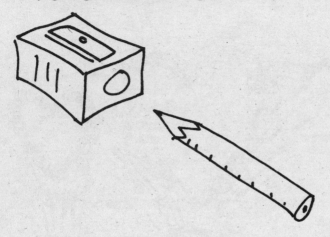

Mother: Why are you crying?
Arabella: Jennifer broke my doll.
Mother: How did she do that?
Arabella: I hit her over the head with it.

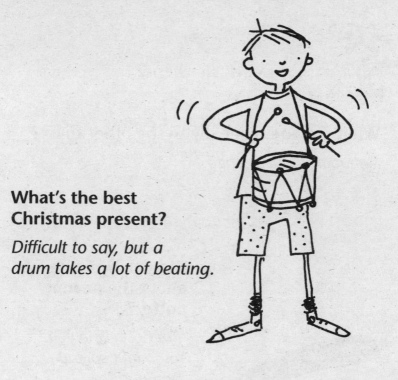

What's the best Christmas present?

Difficult to say, but a drum takes a lot of beating.

Where do baby apes sleep?

In an apricot.

93

What did one toilet say to the other toilet?

'You look a little flushed.'

Did you hear the joke about the peanut butter?

'I'm not telling you. You might spread it around!'

How do you start a teddy-bear race?

'Ready, teddy, go!'

Why are teddy bears never hungry?

They're always stuffed.

What's the wettest animal in the world?

A reindeer.

What do you call a reindeer with no eyes?

No idea.

What do you call a reindeer with no eyes and no legs?

Still no idea.

What do you call a reindeer with a number plate on its rump?

Reg.

What game do four reindeer play in the back of a Mini?

Squash.

Why are reindeer such bad dancers?

They have two left feet.

What's bugging Jack?

One day Jack answered the door to find a huge cockroach standing on the doorstep. The cockroach made a horrible face at Jack, twisted his arm, then ran off.

The next day, the doorbell rang again, and Jack found the same massive cockroach standing at his door. The huge hissing insect hit him in the face, then scurried away before Jack could do anything.

On the third day, the cockroach called round again. This time, he called Jack horrible names and kicked him hard on the leg before running away.

Jack was in quite a lot of pain by now, so he decided to go and see his doctor. He explained what had happened on the previous three days. 'Is there anything I can do, Doctor?' he asked.

'I'm afraid not,' said the doctor. 'There's just a nasty bug going round.'

Knock, knock.
Who's there?
Witches.
Witches who?
Witches the way home, please?

Knock, knock.
Who's there?
Radio.
Radio who?
Radio not, here I come!

Knock, knock.
Who's there?
Tank!
Tank who?
You're welcome!

Knock, knock.
Who's there?
Felix.
Felix who?
Felix my ice cream again, I'll bash him!

Pupil: Miss, would you punish someone for something they didn't do?

Teacher: Of course not!

Pupil: Oh good, because I haven't done my homework.

Teacher: You know you really should become an underwater photographer one day.

Pupil: Why, sir?

Teacher: Because all your grades are below 'C' level.

Teacher: You missed school yesterday, didn't you?

Pupil: Er, not very much!

What runs round Santa's reindeer paddock without moving?

The fence.

What's a snake's favourite subject at school?

Hiss-tory.

Where does a three-metre-tall polar bear sleep?

Anywhere it wants to.

105

Why were the ancient Egyptians confused?

Because their daddies were mummies!

What did the frog order at the restaurant?

French flies and a can of Croak.

Why did the frog say 'miaow'?

He was learning a foreign language.

Why do dragons sleep during the day?

So they can fight knights.

A String Thing

Two pieces of string met one day in the park. One had a go on the slide while the other one went on the swings. They were having a great time until the first piece of string decided to go on the roundabout. After a while he started to feel dizzy, then suddenly he fell off, ending up in a big tangled heap on the ground and getting a bit unravelled.

The second piece of string looked at him and said, 'You're not very good on that roundabout, are you?'

The first piece of string looked at himself and said, 'I'm a frayed knot.'

How do monkeys make toast?

They put the bread under a gorilla.

Why did the banana go to the doctor?

He wasn't peeling very well.

Did you hear about the man who was tap-dancing?

He broke his ankle when he fell into the sink.

What's big, grey, heavy and wears glass slippers?

Cinderella-phant.

What did Cinderella say when her photos didn't arrive?

'Someday my prints will come.'

What has four wheels and flies?

A rubbish truck.

Did you hear the one about the magic tractor?

It went down the road and turned into a field!

Why do bicycles fall over?

Because they are two-tyred.

What time do you go to the dentist?

Tooth-hurty.

What do elves learn in school?

The elf-abet.

How did the music teacher get locked in the classroom?

Her keys were inside the piano.

Why were the teacher's eyes crossed?

She couldn't control her pupils.

Why did the music teacher need a ladder?

To reach the high notes.

Teacher: If I had thirty bananas in one hand and twenty bananas in the other, what would I have?

Pupil: Er, very big hands?

Knock, knock.
Who's there.
Canoe.
Canoe who?
Canoe help me with my homework? I'm stuck!

Knock, knock.
Who's there?
A titch.
A titch who?
Bless you!

Knock, knock.
Who's there?
Emma.
Emma who?
Emma bit cold out here, will you let me in?

Knock, knock.
Who's there?
Twit.
Twit who?
You sound like an owl!

There once was a Viking named Rudolph the Red. He was at home one day with his wife. He looked out of the window and said, 'Look, darling, it's raining.'

She shook her head. 'I don't think so, dear. I think it's snowing.'

But Rudolph knew better, so he said, 'Let's go outside and we'll find out.'

They went outside and discovered that it was in fact raining. And Rudolph turned to his wife and said, 'I knew it was raining. Rudolph the Red knows rain, dear!'

Knock, knock.
Who's there?
Wenceslas.
Wenceslas who?
Wenceslas bus home on Christmas Eve?

Inflatable Fun

There once was an inflatable boy who didn't like going to his inflatable school. One day he was feeling particularly naughty, so when he saw the inflatable headmaster approaching him in the corridor, he pulled out a large pin and pricked him, letting all his air out. The boy ran out of the inflatable school gates and, as he did so, he pulled out his pin and punctured the inflatable school. Then he ran all the way back to his inflatable home.

That evening, the inflatable police turned up at his house, and when he saw them arriving at the door, the inflatable boy panicked! He pulled out his pin again and jabbed it into himself.

The next day, the inflatable boy woke up in an inflatable hospital and, by an amazing coincidence, he found the inflatable headmaster lying in the hospital bed next to him.

When he saw the inflatable boy, the inflatable headmaster shook his head sadly and said to him, 'Well, my boy, you've let me down, you've let the school down, but, worst of all, you've let yourself down.'

What is a ghost's favourite position in football?

Ghoul-keeper.

'Doctor, doctor, I keep thinking I'm a bridge!'

'What's come over you?'

'Two lorries, three cars and a bike.'

Why did the fly fly?

Because the spider spied 'er.

**Where does Santa stay
when he's on holiday?**

At a ho-ho-hotel!

**What are a monkey's
favourite snacks?**

Chocolate-chimp cookies.

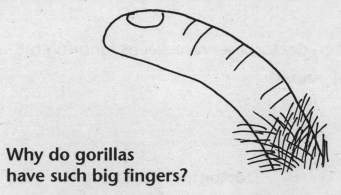

**Why do gorillas
have such big fingers?**

Have you seen the size of their noses?

'Doctor, doctor, I keep thinking I'm invisible!'

'Did someone say something?'

'Doctor, doctor, everyone keeps ignoring me.'

'Next, please!'

'Doctor, doctor, I keep thinking I'm a pack of cards.'

'I'll deal with you later.'

'Doctor, doctor, I keep thinking I'm a snooker ball.'

'So that's why you're at the end of the queue.'

'Doctor, doctor, I keep thinking I'm a pair of curtains.'

'Well, pull yourself together!'

Mum, can I have a dog for Christmas?

No, you can have turkey like everyone else.

How does Rudolph know when Christmas is coming?

He looks at his calen-deer.

What kind of cake does Frosty the Snowman like?

Any kind, as long as it has lots of icing.

What does Santa get if he's stuck in a chimney?

Claustrophobic.

'Doctor, doctor, I keep thinking I'm a goat.'
'And how long has this been going on?'
'Ever since I was a kid.'

Why did the chicken cross the road?

To get to the other side.

Why did the cow cross the road?

To get to the udder side.

Why did the horse cross the road?

It was the chicken's day off.

129

Why did the chicken cross the playground?

To get to the other slide.

Why did the turkey cross the road?

To prove he wasn't chicken.

If I'm standing at the North Pole, facing the South Pole, and the east is on my left, what's on my right hand?

Fingers.

What did the bald man say when he got a comb for Christmas?

'Thanks, I'll never part with it.'

Who delivers Christmas presents to dogs?

Santa Paws.

Knock, knock.
Who's there?
Major.
Major who?
Major open the door, didn't I?

Knock, knock.
Who's there?
Hairy.
Hairy who?
Hairy up and let me in.

Knock, knock.
Who's there?
Doughnut.
Doughnut who?
Doughnut ask me any more silly questions.

Knock, knock.
Who's there?
Lego.
Lego who?
Lego of me and I'll tell you.

How do you make a milkshake?

Give it a good scare.

Which cheese is made backwards?

Edam.

What kind of cheese doesn't belong to you?

Nacho cheese!

What kind of cheese would you use to disguise a horse?

Mascarpone!

What do you call a peanut in a spacesuit?

An astronut.

When do astronauts eat?

At launch-time.

What washes up on very small beaches?

Microwaves.

Why did the golfer wear two pairs of pants?

In case he got a hole in one.

What's purple and about 4,000 miles long?

The Grape Wall of China.

What did one wall say to the other wall?

'I'll meet you at the corner.'

Why did the ballerina quit?

Because it was tutu hard.

David: Have you bought your grandmother's Christmas present yet, Susie?

Susie: No. I was going to get her a handkerchief, but I changed my mind.

David: Why?

Susie: I can't work out what size her nose is.

What's the best thing to put into your Christmas dinner?

Your teeth.

What do you call a boomerang that doesn't work?

A stick.

What do ghosts eat for dinner?

Spook-etti.

How does a witch tell the time?

She looks at her witch-watch.

What does a ghost call his parents?

Mum and Dead.

What's a ghost's favourite day of the week?

Fright-day.

How do skeletons keep in touch with each other?

By mobile bone.

What does a dragon call a knight in armour?

Tinned food.

What do you give a seasick monster?

Plenty of room.

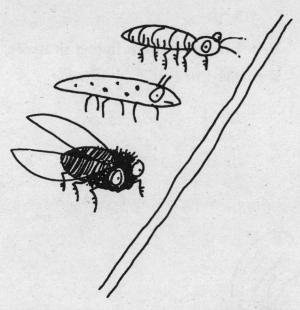

How do you start an insect race?

'One, two, flea, go!'

How do you catch a squirrel?

Climb up a tree and act like a nut.

What do you call a flying skunk?

A smellicopter.

What goes 'zzub, zzub'?

A bee flying backwards.

How do you make a sausage roll?

Give it a push.

Did you hear about the polar bear who tried to eat a penguin?

He couldn't get the wrapper off.

What sort of ball doesn't bounce?

A snowball.

What did the traffic light say to the car?

'Don't look, I'm changing!'

What's the best thing to give your parents at Christmas?

A list of everything you want.

Pizza Fit for a King

Good King Wenceslas looked out of his window at the thick snow. It was too cold to go outside and he was feeling very hungry. Suddenly he had a great idea. He would phone for a pizza and get it delivered! Quickly he made the call and ordered himself a large cheese and tomato pizza.

'How would you like it?' asked the pizza delivery boy.

'Deep pan, crisp and even!' replied Good King Wenceslas.

What do you get if you pour boiling water down a rabbit hole?

Hot cross bunnies.

Why was the toilet paper rolling down the hill?

To get to the bottom.

Why do bees hum?

Because they always forget the words.

Why do pelicans need lots of money?

Because they have big bills.

What do you call a volcano?

A mountain with hiccups.

What did the octopus say when he played a trick on his friend?

'I was just pulling your leg, leg, leg, leg, leg, leg, leg, leg!'

What does Frosty the Snowman like to put on his icebergers?

Chilly sauce.

What goes, 'Oh oh oh'?

Santa Claus walking backwards!

Who sings 'Love Me Tender' and makes Christmas toys?

Santa's Elvis.

What do you call a sleeping dinosaur?

A dino-snore.

Why do people avoid dinosaurs?

Because their eggs stink.

Knock, knock.
Who's there?
Granny.
Granny who?
Knock, knock.
Who's there?
Granny.
Granny who?
Knock, knock.
Who's there?
Granny.
Granny who?
Knock, knock
Who's there?
Aunt.
Aunt who?
Aunt you glad I got rid of all those grannies?

Christmas Poems

Chosen by Gaby Morgan

Decorated by Axel Scheffler

The holly and the ivy,
When they are both full grown,
Of all the trees that are in the wood,
The holly bears the crown.

This festive collection of classic and brand-new poems
celebrates all the best things about Christmas from the Nativity
to Father Christmas, including snow, angels, reindeer,
Christmas trees and, of course, Mary, Joseph and baby Jesus.

Christmas Jokes

What do you call a smelly Santa?

Farter Christmas!

What do reindeer always say before telling a joke?

This one will sleigh you!

Tickle your funny bone with this must-have collection of Christmas jokes. Full of seasonal silliness and festive fun, you'd have to be **Christmas crackers** to miss it!